Wounded Knee

WOUNDED KNEE

The Death of a Dream

LAURIE A. O'NEILL

Spotlight on American History
The Millbrook Press • Brookfield, Connecticut

Cover: A buckskin painting of the Ghost Dance ritual, on file in the picture library of the Smithsonian Institution.

Map by Joe Le Monnier

Photographs courtesy of Smithsonian Institution: pp. 10 (both), 28, 37, 41, 52, 56; Buffalo Bill Historical Society: pp. 13, 21; Thomas Gilcrease Museum: p. 17; Henry E. Huntington Library: p. 25; National Archives: pp. 31, 45; Bettmann Archive: pp. 33, 39, 46; Library of Congress: cover, p. 50.

Library of Congress Cataloging-in-Publication Data
O'Neill, Laurie, 1949–
Wounded Knee/The Death of a dream/by Laurie O'Neill.
A Millbrook Press library ed.
p.   cm.—(Spotlight on American history)
Includes bibliographical references and index.
Summary: Examines the bloody confrontation at Wounded Knee, South Dakota in 1890 between U.S. Cavalry troops and the Sioux Indians.
ISBN 1-56294-253-0 (lib. bdg.)
1. Wounded Knee Creek, Battle of, 1890—Juvenile literature.   2. Dakota Indians—Wars, 1890–1891—Juvenile literature.   3. Dakota Indians—History—19th century—Juvenile literature.   4. Dakota Indians—Government relations—Juvenile literature.
[1. Wounded Knee Creek, Battle of, 1890.   2. Dakota Indians—Wars, 1890–1891.   3. Indians of North America—Wars.]   I. Title.   II. Series.
E83.89.O54   1993   973.8'6—dc20   92-12998   CIP   AC

Published by The Millbrook Press
2 Old New Milford Road, Brookfield, Connecticut 06804

Contents

To Colin

CANADA

Missouri River

NORTH DAKOTA

Standing Rock Agency ●

Yellowstone River

Little Missouri River

✕ Battle of Little Bighorn

MONTANA

✕ Sitting Bull Killed

Missouri River

■ Ft. C.F. Smith

SOUTH DAKOTA

Belle Fourche River

✕ Fetterman Incident

Cheyenne River Agency ●

■ Ft. Phil Kearny

BLACK HILLS

Cheyenne River

White River

BADLANDS

✕ Wounded Knee

Pine Ridge Reservation ●

WYOMING

R O C K Y   M O U N T A I N S

✕ Grattan Incident

NEBRASKA

UTAH

COLORADO

KANSAS

Legend

✕	Conflicts
■	U.S. Army Forts
●	Indian Agencies

0 — 100 Miles

0 — 150 Kilometers

1

DEATH AT WOUNDED KNEE

To Native Americans, few words bring forth such a strong emotional response as Wounded Knee. Wounded Knee Creek, on the Pine Ridge Reservation in southwestern South Dakota, was the site of a bloody confrontation between a peaceful band of Sioux Indians and U.S. cavalry troops on December 29, 1890. When it was over, an estimated two hundred Lakota Sioux men, women, and children were dead or wounded.

The U.S. government was quick to call the incident a battle. But the Sioux knew otherwise. To them, the violence had only one name: the Wounded Knee Massacre.

On that bitterly cold winter morning, the tension could be felt as the Seventh Cavalry guarded 350 Sioux, camped in a narrow valley along Wounded Knee Creek. The Indians were followers of Chief Big Foot, the aged leader of a subtribe of Lakota called Miniconjou. He lay ill with pneumonia, weak and breathing with difficulty, in an army tent. At Big Foot's request, a white flag of peace fluttered from the center of the Indian camp.

Chief Big Foot was old and sick by the time he arrived at Wounded Knee, but this photograph, taken in 1872, shows a strong and determined leader.

The Seventh Cavalry camp at Wounded Knee, South Dakota. This photograph was taken before the soldiers turned on Big Foot's band, killing or wounding hundreds of Lakota Sioux.

Completely surrounding the Indians were nearly five hundred soldiers of the U.S. Seventh Cavalry. They were dressed in crisp blue uniforms with bright brass buttons. Many were mounted on sleek, blanketed cavalry horses. The soldiers had set up four powerful Hotchkiss guns on a ridge, pointed directly at the Indian camp. These guns were capable of hurling 2-pound (0.9-kilogram) explosive shells at the rate of fifty per minute.

Probably neither side expected violence. Big Foot and his followers, poorly armed and exhausted from their winter journey, had been on their way from the Miniconjou village on the Cheyenne River Reservation to the Indian agency (the administrative headquarters) at Pine Ridge, roughly a 150-mile (241-kilometer) trip. Big Foot had planned to join Red Cloud, another Lakota Sioux chief, there. Both men wanted peace with the U.S. government.

However, army troops were sent to round up Big Foot—who was viewed as a troublemaker by the government—and his band. On December 28, Major Samuel M. Whitside tracked Big Foot down only 20 miles (32 kilometers) from the chief's destination and ordered him to surrender. The Sioux were then marched to the soldiers' camp at Wounded Knee.

During the night another cavalry officer, Colonel James W. Forsyth, arrived with reinforcements and took over command of the operation. Early the next morning, after reveille had been sounded and breakfast rations distributed, Forsyth told the Sioux men to form a long line facing the cavalry. Then he sent them in small groups to their tipis to retrieve any guns, knives, or clubs they might have.

The process of disarming the Sioux was slow because the Indians, fearing the loss of their only means of protection, were reluctant to give up their guns. Forsyth grew impatient. He sent his officers into the tipis to look for weapons.

While the soldiers ransacked the tipis, pushing the women and children aside, the Sioux men became nervous. A medicine man named Yellow Bird began urging his people to resist. He chanted in the Lakota Sioux language, blew on his eagle-bone whistle, and tossed handfuls of dust into the air. Yellow Bird raised his arms and pointed to his brightly decorated shirt. Similar garments were worn by others in the group. These shirts, Yellow Bird reminded them, represented the Ghost Spirits who would protect the Indians from the soldiers' bullets.

A search of the tipis produced only a small number of guns. Forsyth grew suspicious. Believing the Sioux had more weapons, he ordered the Indian men to remove the blankets they had wrapped themselves in for protection against the numbing cold.

Trouble began when the soldiers tried to take a new rifle away from a young Sioux named Black Coyote, who was deaf. A scuffle broke out, and the rifle discharged a shot into the air. Uneasy and tense throughout the search, the soldiers immediately opened fire at close range, cutting down dozens of Sioux within seconds. Some of Big Foot's men scrambled to retrieve their weapons. Even the women tried desperately to fight off the soldiers with their fists.

Suddenly, cannon fire burst from the ridge, and the exploding shells tore into the Indian camp, reducing the tipis and any Sioux still in them to burning shreds. Many Sioux sought protection in a dry, shallow ravine that ran west of the creek, but the soldiers fired down on them. It was a scene of horror: smoke, dust, flying bullets, explosions, and confusion.

Within only minutes, at least 150 Sioux were dead. Many more lay wounded and maimed. Big Foot had been killed in the opening fire. About twenty-five soldiers had died, most, it is said, in the cross fire from their own regiment.

*Bodies lie strewn about in the snow after what the
U.S. government called "the battle at Wounded Knee"
and the Sioux called the "massacre."*

After the massacre, army wagons moved over the valley, picking up dead and injured cavalrymen. About fifty wounded Sioux, nearly all of them women and children, were loaded into wagons and taken to the army barracks at Pine Ridge. That night the snowstorm that had threatened all day developed into a raging blizzard. The wind howled, the snow swirled, and soon a white blanket covered the bloody field. The eerie quiet was broken only by the anguished wailing of a Sioux woman, standing on the ridge.

A holy man named Black Elk, from the Lakota subtribe of Oglalas, had been camped on the reservation and had heard the gunfire. When the blizzard ended, he rode to Wounded Knee. As he viewed the frozen bodies of his people strewn over the valley, he felt a searing pain inside.

Years later he would look down from that ridge and "still see the butchered women and children lying heaped and scattered all along the crooked gulch as plain as when [he] saw them with eyes still young." And he saw "that something else died there in the bloody mud and was buried in the blizzard. A people's dream died there. It was a beautiful dream."

What was the dream that died that winter morning in South Dakota? To understand what led to the Wounded Knee Massacre, one must look back to the beginning of the long struggle between the Native American people and the soldiers and settlers who had set out to win the West, a struggle that would become one of the darkest chapters in U.S. history.

PLAINS DWELLERS

*T*he *Great Plains* of North America is a region that extends from northern Canada to south Texas. One million square miles (nearly 2.6 million square kilometers) in area, the region is bordered in the United States by the Mississippi River in the east and the Rocky Mountains in the west. It was the scene of the final conflicts between Native Americans and the United States in the late 1800s.

Mostly dry, dusty, and treeless except in its river valleys, the Great Plains region is a vast sea of grass. In some places, highlands rise dramatically from the plains, with imposing sandstone, limestone, and granite outcroppings and towering pine trees. One such area is the Black Hills of South Dakota and Wyoming. Named for its thick growths of dark green pine trees, it is considered a sacred place by the Sioux; they call it Paha-Sapa.

Other highland areas are barren, eroding hills with weird rock formations and dark caves and canyons. The Badlands of South Dakota were thought by the Plains Indians to be haunted.

The Sioux reached the Plains in the early 1700s, migrating from the lakes region at the head of the Mississippi River. Originally forest dwellers, the Sioux were forced to move west, across the Missouri River, when their traditional enemies, the Chippewas, obtained guns from French traders and became more dangerous. It was the Chippewas who gave the Sioux their name. They used the word *Nadewisue* to describe their enemies. In the Algonquian language used by the Chippewas, this word means adder, a kind of snake.

As the Sioux arrived on the Plains, they were met with an astonishing sight: herds of bison, or buffalo. There were millions of the shaggy beasts, blackening the landscape as far as the eye could see. Soon these creatures would become the center of Sioux life, providing nearly everything necessary for survival.

The Sioux called themselves Dakota, which means "many in one," or "allies." The Dakota was the largest Plains tribe. It was made up of four major geographical groups: Teton, Santee, Yankton, and Yanktonai. Ranging farthest west were the Tetons—their name means "dwellers on the plains." They called themselves Lakota and claimed the Black Hills area as their homeland.

Of all the North American Indian groups, the Lakotas are the people we most often think of when picturing Native Americans of the nineteenth-century West. Roaming freely over the Plains, living in tipis, hunting buffalo, riding horseback, and dressed in colorful garments decorated with beads and eagle feathers, this tribe produced such great historic figures as Sitting Bull and Crazy Horse.

The Lakotas were made up of seven subgroups: Hunkpapas, Miniconjous, Oglalas, Blackfeet, Brulés, San Arcs, and Two Kettles. The first three groups figure prominently in the Wounded Knee

*Despite the harsh weather and barren prairie, the Sioux
thrived on the Great Plains throughout the 1700s and early
1800s when herds of buffalo still roamed the land.*

story. A subgroup included many bands of Sioux. These bands usually represented large extended families of relatives and friends, each led by one chief.

Although respected as advisers, military leaders, powerful healers, and prophets, the chiefs did not speak for all the native peoples—not even for their own tribe, subgroup, or band. They did not make any major decisions without consulting the older males of the group.

Once on the Plains, the Sioux had to adapt to their new environment. Unlike the lush forests from which they had come, this land was desertlike and subject to harsh weather. Icy winds would lower the temperature dramatically in winter; in summer there were searing blasts of hot air. There could be severe storms. The sun was fierce and relentless.

But there were great herds of buffalo, which the Sioux, deeply religious, believed were provided to them by the Great Spirit, whom they called Wakan Tanka. With this blessing they would be able to survive in this strange new land.

FOLLOWING THE HERDS

At first the Sioux hunted buffalo on foot, using bows and arrows or spears. Later they acquired guns from French and English traders. The Sioux became a nomadic, or wandering, people, living in buffalo-hide tipis that could be set up or taken down in minutes. They followed the herds in spring and summer, as the buffalo spread out on the Plains to graze.

In late autumn, when the frigid Arctic winds began to blow across the flatland, the great herds divided into smaller ones to find food and winter cover. So did the Sioux tribes, separating into bands and seeking shelter in wooded valleys. They piled buffalo robes on their tipis for warmth, ate sun-dried buffalo meat, and hunted for deer, elk, and smaller game.

Each spring the bands would come together, camping in a huge circle. Friendships would be renewed, and feasting, singing, and dancing would be enjoyed. Prayer was central to the spiritual life of the Sioux. They prayed for the buffalo to return in the spring. Days of ritual preceded each hunt.

A buffalo, which weighed approximately 1,800 pounds (817 kilograms), could feed many people. Although much of the meat was consumed immediately, some was sun-dried and mixed with berries and buffalo fat, resulting in a sort of high-energy food called pemmican.

The Sioux, like all native peoples, possessed a deep respect for all living things and a belief that none of the earth's resources should be wasted. Every part of the buffalo was used. Skins became robes, blankets, shirts, leggings, moccasins, and tipi covers. Rawhide strips were used as rope or string, for attaching stone tools to wood handles, and, when the Sioux acquired horses, as leads and reins. Sinew, or tendon, was used as sewing thread. The bones and horns were fashioned into arrowheads and cooking utensils. The blood of the buffalo became face paint. Even the stomach and bladder were used, as containers for water.

When the Sioux acquired horses, their way of life changed. The horse, extinct in North America for centuries, was reintroduced by the Spanish in the 1600s. The creatures slowly began to show up in southern and then northern Plains tribes. By 1750 most Plains Indians had them.

The Sioux became expert riders. The horse allowed them to be better hunters and to travel hundreds of miles each spring, summer, and fall. Now they could journey farther to trade their buffalo hides for such goods as beads, cloth, metal, coffee, sugar, matches, guns, and ammunition. No longer did they have to transport their tipis and other belongings on their backs or pull a travois (pronounced *tra-voy*), a framework of poles and hides dragged along the ground by a member of the tribe. Now horses carried the heavy loads and pulled the travois.

Even the most expert rider was in danger during a buffalo hunt, as this famous painting by Frederic Remington shows.

Intertribal warfare was an important part of Sioux life. Raids on enemy camps were made to capture horses, as revenge for theft, or as punishment for intrusion on a tribe's hunting grounds. The horse was a sign of wealth to the Sioux. Some tribal leaders owned hundreds of the animals.

The Indians fought each other for personal glory. Bravery in battle was the standard by which young Indian men were judged. Individual honor was every warrior's goal. One way to earn honor was to get close enough to an enemy to touch him with a hand or with a special, decorated lance without harming him. This was called "counting coup" (pronounced *coo*).

By the early 1800s the Sioux were self-sufficient and living in harmony with the world around them. It would not be long, however, before the Sioux way of life would be threatened. The Indians would begin a long, desperate fight to hold on to their cherished homeland. To the east, interest in the boundless lands beyond the frontier began to build. A young nation, eager to grow, looked westward.

4

INTRUDERS FROM
THE EAST

For a long time colonists from England and other parts of Europe, settling on the East coast, had not been interested in the Plains. The Spanish feared the Indians; the French and English came to trade but felt the land belonged to the Indians and was unconquerable. American explorers in the early 1800s found a scarcity of wood and water, a harsh climate, and strange inhabitants on the Plains who they believed were wild and dangerous. The Plains, it was agreed, were unfit for settlement.

The United States established an Indian frontier west of the Mississippi River, and in the 1820s and 1830s, many eastern tribes were forced to relocate there as settlers took over their land. Soon the government decided that, even though it did not yet wish to settle the Plains, it would be necessary to cross Indian country to reach the mining, trapping, and farming land of California and Oregon.

Routes across the Plains were created, including the Santa Fe Trail and the Oregon Trail, both of which originated near present-day Kansas City, Missouri. Trading posts were built, and occasional mule trains made their way west. For several years the Indians tolerated these trespassers, even becoming friendly with some of the early trappers and explorers and serving as their guides. At first the travelers, finding the journey difficult, discouraged others from following.

But in the 1840s large numbers of Americans began to feel it was their country's "manifest destiny" (something that was meant to be) to dominate all of North America. Settlers began pushing westward, seeking home and fortune in this land of opportunity. Gold was discovered in California, and prospectors streamed across the Plains by the thousands. Miles of wagons crept west, filled with farmers and ranchers, their families, and supplies, including building materials, livestock, and fencing.

Clashes with the Plains Indians were inevitable. The Native Americans watched in horror as their homeland was invaded, the grassland trampled, the earth rutted and littered, and the buffalo frightened and driven from their grazing areas. The settlers did not understand or respect the Indians' native rights to the land. They saw these Plains inhabitants as savages rather than real people and wanted to drive them away.

Reacting to the intruders with confusion, alarm, and anger, the Indians tried to scare off the settlers and defend their land. The settlers fought back, sometimes shooting any Indian on sight. Bloody Indian attacks on white settlements were actually rare, and accounts of those that occurred were exaggerated back East. Such reporting helped form the unfortunate stereotypes that in some American minds still persist: Native Americans as bloodthirsty savages, white settlers as brave pioneers and patriots.

Taking advantage of the newly created trails across the plains,
settlers and gold prospectors came with their wagons, guns, and
absolute conviction that it was their right to occupy Indian lands.

The settlers demanded protection, and the government sent troops of infantry and cavalry to the frontier. The military began buying trading posts on the Plains, turning them into army forts filled with blue-coated troops and supplies of arms and ammunition.

Several treaties, or agreements, were made between the U.S. government and Native Americans from the 1850s through the 1870s.

Government representatives convinced tribes to give up portions of their hunting grounds in exchange for promises of food, clothing, supplies, and annual payments for their lost land. With each treaty, the Indians were promised that they would be left alone to live forever as they pleased on their remaining land.

The Indians, however, were taken advantage of by government representatives. They were often cheated out of their land when a chief was pressured, sometimes with the use of alcohol, to sign a treaty.

The westward flow of settlers continued. Convinced that the Indians were in the way of progress, the government decided they must be moved onto reservations, which were isolated areas of land put aside for them to live on. In 1849 a government agent was sent west to arrange a meeting with the northern Plains tribes, including the Lakotas. The meeting led to a huge conference in 1851 near Fort Laramie in present-day Wyoming, at which some ten thousand Indians gathered. Although many of the tribes were traditional enemies, they had called a truce for the conference. Still, hundreds of soldiers stood ready in case of trouble.

The government asked the tribes to stay within specific boundaries, away from the settlers' routes. In return, the Indians were guaranteed protection from the settlers and promised annual payments of $50,000 for several years.

Swayed with talk of generous rations of food and supplies, including guns, most of the Indians agreed to the terms of the treaty. For several months there was peace on the Plains.

But the numbers of settlers steadily increased. They brought diseases, including smallpox, typhus, influenza, and cholera. The Indians had no immunities to these strange ailments, and entire tribes were nearly wiped out. Cattle took over the buffalo's grazing land. Trees from the Indians' beloved hills were cut for timber. Relations between the settlers and the Indians became increasingly tense.

In 1854 a group of Mormon settlers was traveling west on the Oregon Trail. They lost a cow, which wandered into a Brulé Lakota camp. Although the animal was sickly and very thin, the Indians, faced with hunger due to the greatly reduced supply of buffalo, killed and ate it. Reporting the "theft" at Fort Laramie, the cow's owner demanded justice.

The young Brulé who had butchered the cow took refuge in the camp of Chief Conquering Bear. The government had designated Conquering Bear the spokesman for all the Lakotas, although this was a position the Sioux did not recognize. The chief went to the fort to pay for the cow, but the owner demanded more than twice the amount Conquering Bear offered. The chief said this was too much to pay for a lame, sickly animal. Conquering Bear returned to his camp.

Meanwhile, a young army officer, Second Lieutenant John L. Grattan, felt the incident called for military action. Boasting that he could "wipe out" the Indians with just thirty men, he headed to the camp with thirty soldiers and two cannons. There, Conquering Bear tried to discuss the matter with Grattan. Without warning, the officer turned and ordered his company to fire on the camp. Conquering Bear was mortally wounded in the first volley of shots. The Sioux rushed to defend themselves, killing Grattan and all his men.

In the East the incident was falsely reported as a massacre by "treacherous" Indians. The next summer Colonel William S. Harney was ordered to teach the Sioux a lesson. With more than a thousand men, he marched into a Brulé camp, assuming wrongly

Conquering Bear, who was killed in 1854 by U.S. soldiers during an argument over a cow.

that it was the same one where the cow had been killed. He demanded Grattan's killers. As the chief turned to warn his people, Harney attacked, killing eighty-six Sioux men and capturing seventy women and children.

This was a turning point in U.S.-Indian relations on the frontier. Most Sioux were now embittered. They had trusted the government, yet the Indians' land was being seized despite treaty promises. The government, however, felt that more needed to be done to free up the western lands for settlement. The Plains Indians, it was decided, must be eliminated.

5

WAR ON THE PLAINS

Dozens of battles and skirmishes marked the next twenty-five years, and violence was nearly constant on the Plains. The fighting was fierce. Some of the military campaigns were conducted in blizzards or subzero temperatures. Many of the U.S. troops, particularly the officers, were Civil War veterans. Nearly one fifth of the soldiers sent to the frontier were black. Some Indians, believing that the army would eventually conquer them, fought on the side of the United States or served as scouts or as tribal police on the uneasy reservations.

Between the 1860s and 1890s, thousands of Native Americans were forced onto reservations. Many, however, continued to resist the loss of their land and fought to preserve their way of life on the Plains. In 1863 the War for the Bozeman Trail, or Red Cloud's War, began.

The Bozeman Trail was a new, more direct route west. It ran right through Powder River Country, the Indian territory around the Yellowstone River in what is now Montana. Angry Sioux began attacking wagon trains and army detachments, and the military sent reinforcements to its forts.

During the autumn of 1865, the attacks continued on work parties gathering hay and timber outside the forts. Captain William J. Fetterman wanted to put an end to the problem. "Give me eighty men and I will ride through the whole Indian nation!" he boasted. Soon after, Fetterman and eighty men rode into an ambush of Sioux while attempting a surprise attack on the Indians. He and all his men died.

After the Fetterman incident, more soldiers were sent to the frontier with new, breech-loading rifles, which could be fired more rapidly than older models. Two major skirmishes took place in 1867, near Fort C. F. Smith in Montana and Fort Phil Kearny in Wyoming. Many Sioux were killed, but the Indians managed to drive the soldiers back to their posts.

It was becoming more costly and difficult for the government to keep the Bozeman Trail open. At Fort Laramie a new treaty was introduced. The Sioux would be asked to move onto a reservation that included all of South Dakota west of the Missouri River. It would be called the Great Sioux Reservation, and the government agreed to build schools, sawmills, and other facilities there and to provide the Sioux with food and clothing.

In turn the Sioux were to stop harassing the settlers and allow the construction of railroads across the Plains. A large area of land outside the reservation was declared unceded Indian territory, which meant the Sioux could continue to hunt there and no settlers would be allowed in the area.

Some Indians signed the treaty in April 1868, but Red Cloud and others refused. They wanted the government to close the Bozeman Trail and the three forts along it and to leave the Powder River Country alone. After continued attacks on army detach-

This photograph shows the signing of the 1868 treaty that would move the Sioux onto a reservation and allow settlement to continue on their lands. Red Cloud refused to sign.

ments, the government finally agreed, and the trail and forts were abandoned. The Indians considered this a major victory.

Peace prevailed for a time, but soon the government desired yet another piece of Indian land, for construction of the Northern Pacific Railway. Expeditions of surveyors and explorers, escorted by soldiers, were made into the Black Hills during the early 1870s. They planned not only to determine the location of the railway, but also to find a site for a new fort and to decide if the soil was suitable for farming.

One of these expeditions was led in 1874 by a former army general, George Armstrong Custer. An ambitious glory seeker who hoped to be president of the United States one day, Custer was a notorious Indian hater. Six years earlier he had commanded the Seventh Cavalry in a surprise attack on a peaceful Cheyenne village in Oklahoma, killing even the Indians' horses and dogs.

Custer confirmed that the Black Hills were rich in gold, and his well-publicized discovery triggered a massive gold rush west. Although Custer's expedition into the Black Hills violated the 1868 treaty, the Sioux did not go to war against the intruders. But they had a new name for Lieutenant Colonel Custer, whom they had called Long Hair for his golden shoulder-length tresses. Now he would be known as Chief of Thieves.

The government sent representatives in 1875 to make a deal with the Sioux to purchase or lease the Black Hills. The Indians were horrified. The Black Hills, they believed, could not be bought or sold. This was their sacred place. The meeting was a failure. Angered, the government tried to push all Indians onto reservations and to make them abandon their nomadic ways and become farmers.

One way to force the Indians into submission would be to take away their source of life: the buffalo. Although the great herds had already been significantly reduced, the extermination of the remaining buffalo began, and the government did nothing to stop it. Hunting parties, some equipped with telescopic sights on their high-powered rifles, swept over the Plains, killing the creatures for their hides or simply for sport. Travelers on trains often fired at buffalo from their windows for amusement.

Railway construction crews killed countless numbers of the animals. One crew was supervised by William F. Cody, whose skill

*The Sioux called
George Armstrong
Custer, Long Hair.
After he violated
the 1868 treaty,
he became known as
Chief of Thieves.*

with a rifle earned him the nickname Buffalo Bill. Unlike the Sioux, who did not waste any part of a buffalo, these hunters wanted only the hides or sometimes the tongue, which was considered a delicacy. At the peak of the mass slaughter, buffalo carcasses lay rotting in the sun for miles.

Without the buffalo, the Indians were deprived of their principal food source and gradually forced to abandon their way of life as nomadic hunters. As they were pressed onto reservation land, a few of their leaders still vowed to remain free. One was the Hunkpapa chief and holy man Sitting Bull.

In the Valley of the Greasy Grass, near the Little Bighorn River in Montana, Sitting Bull helped achieve a stunning victory over Lieutenant Colonel Custer on July 25, 1876. With the Oglala chief Crazy Horse, a respected military leader known for his skill and bravery in battle, Sitting Bull led a combined force of some three thousand Lakotas and Cheyennes against U.S. troops.

Within fifteen minutes on that hot, dusty day, Custer and all 225 of his men were killed. Only a horse named Comanche survived the battle. Custer had vastly underestimated the great number of his opponents and charged the Indian camp without waiting for reinforcements. Back East, sympathy lay with Custer and his cavalry, and the incident, known as the Battle of Little Bighorn, was widely viewed as a massacre of U.S. troops. A thirst for revenge began to build, and all Indians were targets.

BROKEN PROMISES

After the Battle of Little Bighorn, the Sioux that refused to move onto the reservation divided into two groups, and the army set out after them. Their leaders, Sitting Bull and Crazy Horse, were ordered to surrender. In the spring of 1877, Sitting Bull and more than two thousand followers, tired of running, crossed the U.S. border into Canada, hoping for protection from the government there.

Late that year Sitting Bull received some terrible news. Crazy Horse, his people sick and near starvation, had surrendered to the U.S. army. Worse, while resisting imprisonment at Fort Robinson in Nebraska, the thirty-five-year-old chief had been killed by a sentry's bayonet.

Sitting Bull was now regarded as one of the last resisters to settlement of the West. Government officials wanted him back in the United States where he could be watched. The chief was offered a pardon for his role at Little Bighorn and promised his own place to live on the reservation, but Sitting Bull refused to consider surrender. As the months passed, reports from the reservation were discouraging. The Sioux were hungry, cold, and desperate. Their guns and most of their horses had been taken away. But Sitting Bull could not remain in Canada much longer. Canada would not provide reservation land or aid for the Sioux. They began to starve. During the winter some of their horses froze to death, and the Sioux were forced to eat them.

Sitting Bull's people began drifting back across the border, most on foot, discouraged and weary. The chief held out until 1881. He finally surrendered with his family and fewer than two hundred remaining followers at Fort Buford, North Dakota, just south of the Canadian border. Instead of being allowed to join his people on the reservation, Sitting Bull was charged with the murder of Custer. He and his followers were taken to Fort Randall and held as prisoners. There Sitting Bull lived quietly, sustained by his memories of the old ways.

In 1882, Sitting Bull was transferred to Standing Rock Agency, in the northernmost section of the Great Sioux Reservation. There, to his dismay, he found his people in thin cloth tipis, their clothing tattered. He continued to encourage his people to resist any further loss of their land and to honor their culture and traditions despite pressure from the government to adopt white people's customs.

The United States was still not satisfied with the progress of settlement on the Plains. An attempt to break up the Great Sioux Reservation into six smaller reservations was made in 1887. The government introduced the Dawes Act, which would free up more territory for white settlement. The Sioux would lose some 100 million acres (nearly 40.5 million hectares), half their land. For two years they protested the plan, counting on the 1868 treaty to protect them. Its terms could be changed only with the consent of three quarters of the adult male Indian population.

After the Battle of Little Bighorn, Sitting Bull fled to Canada. In 1881 he returned to North Dakota where he was arrested and imprisoned for Custer's murder. This 1882 photograph clearly shows his feelings of sadness and defeat.

Soon the government would wait no longer. General George Crook was sent to the reservation. He went from agency to agency, determined to obtain the necessary signatures for a new agreement. Slowly the Indians agreed to give up their land, but it was hardly voluntary. Bullied, bribed, and threatened, the men signed.

Crook reached Standing Rock in July 1889, knowing that Sitting Bull's influence on the Sioux there would make these last signatures difficult to acquire. A meeting with the general was arranged by James McLaughlin, the U.S. agent assigned to Standing Rock. Sitting Bull was not told about the meeting. When he found out, he burst into the gathering, but it was too late. A reporter asked Sitting Bull how he felt about losing so much Indian land. The great chief cried, "Indians! There are no Indians left but me!"

GHOST DANCE TROUBLE

Life on the Indian reservations in the 1880s was filled with suffering. Told to work the land, the Sioux were neither given sufficient tools nor properly taught how to be farmers. The soil was parched and barren; all of the good farming land had been given to the settlers. Droughts and hot summer winds withered the crops the Sioux planted and killed their livestock. The Indians, struggling to survive, were bewildered. How could they become farmers? To the Sioux the earth was sacred and was not meant to be plowed, planted, and used for profit.

The Sioux had no choice now but to be dependent on the government for their survival. Payments for their lost land, however, were reduced or never made, as Congress attempted to cut its budget. Rations were often late and of poor quality. Spoiled meat was common. Many Indians, particularly the old and very young, died.

White missionaries imposed their beliefs on the Indians, attempting to "civilize" them. The Sioux were forced to abandon their religious ceremonies and told to wear clothing like that of the settlers and to cut their long hair. Indian children were sent away from their families to schools at the agencies. They were forbidden to speak their Indian languages and encouraged to turn their backs on their native culture.

The buffalo were gone. Despite one hundred years of tradition, the life of the hunter and warrior was over. Filled with despair, the Sioux looked to the Great Spirit for power to overcome their suffering. The answer came in the form of a new religion.

The construction of the Northern Pacific Railroad
tore a gash through what had once been open prairie,
home to both the wild buffalo and the Plains Indians.

During a solar eclipse on New Year's Day in 1889, a sheep-herder named Wovoka, who belonged to the Paiute tribe in Nevada, fell ill, became delirious, and had a vision in which he was taken up to heaven. In this vision Wovoka saw the dead people of his tribe alive again and at peace, well fed and happy.

Wovoka said he was instructed by God to tell his people to stop fighting and live together in peace. He was to teach them certain prayers, songs, and a special dance. If the Indians did these things faithfully, their dead relatives and friends would be brought back to life, and buffalo would again cover the Plains. All soldiers and settlers would disappear from the earth, and the Indians' homeland would be returned to them.

Wovoka's gospel soon spread to all the Plains tribes. The Indians, particularly the Sioux, were eager to accept a spiritual leader who promised to deliver them from their plight. By the autumn of 1890, all the tribes were performing the new ceremony, which was named the Ghost Dance by the settlers who observed it. At Standing Rock, Sitting Bull had doubts about Wovoka's prophecy, but he realized his people needed a source of hope. He allowed the Ghost Dance religion to be practiced.

During the dance, which could last for several days, Indian men, women, and children formed a circle and shuffled to the right and then to the left, chanting. Faster and faster moved the dancers; louder and louder grew the singing. "You shall see your kindred—E'yayo! The father says so—E'yayo!" they would cry.

The dancers worked themselves into a frenzy, their bodies twitching and shuddering. Suddenly one would leave the circle and fall to the ground, claiming to have had a vision like Wovoka's. The Lakota Sioux added another feature to the new religion: the wearing of fringed and decorated Ghost Shirts. These garments were supposed to protect the wearer from harm.

The Ghost Dance religion was misunderstood by the
settlers, who found the dancing and chanting threatening.

The settlers found the dance frightening. They became alarmed: Were the Indians planning an uprising? At first most of the government agents on the reservations were not concerned. They felt the Ghost Dance was not an act of aggression. Women and children participated in the ritual, and they would never be part of a war dance. Besides, the agents knew the Indians were waiting for the fulfillment of Wovoka's prophecy in the spring.

But soon the fervor of the Ghost Dance threatened the agents' authority on the reservations. In October 1890, a new agent, Daniel E. Royer, arrived at Pine Ridge. Inexperienced and nervous, he was quickly named Young Man Afraid of Indians. Royer saw the Ghost Dance as a hostile act and sent an urgent message to Washington, calling for help to control the Sioux.

Troops were sent west, commanded by Major General John R. Brooke. By mid-November there were soldiers—a total of three thousand—at all the agencies. As the troops arrived, large numbers of Sioux, fearing a war was being planned, fled into the Badlands.

The Indian Bureau in Washington had asked each agent to make a list of Indian troublemakers. On at least one list was the name Sitting Bull. General Nelson A. Miles, at his headquarters in Chicago, called for Sitting Bull's arrest, believing the chief was responsible for the Ghost Dance trouble.

At Standing Rock, Agent McLaughlin assembled forty-three of his tribal police, many of them Hunkpapa Sioux like Sitting Bull. In charge of the arrest were tribal police Lieutenant Henry Bull Head and Sergeant Red Tomahawk. Before dawn on December 15, they entered Sitting Bull's one-room cabin.

Sitting Bull was cooperative. As the police hustled the fifty-nine-year-old chief out the door into a freezing drizzle, an angry crowd that had gathered began protesting his arrest and taunting the police. Some of the onlookers, including Sitting Bull's wife, cried out to the chief, accusing him of cowardice.

Suddenly Sitting Bull changed his mind and tried to pull away from his captors. One of his followers, standing in the crowd, pulled a rifle from under his blanket and shot Lieutenant Bull Head. As Bull Head fell, he fired a shot, which hit Sitting Bull in the back. Within seconds, Red Tomahawk shot Sitting Bull in the head, and the chief collapsed, blood streaming down his face and over his chest. In the struggle that followed, eight Sioux, including Sitting Bull's teenage son, Crowfoot, and six policemen, were killed.

8

THE FATEFUL JOURNEY

With Sitting Bull dead the army focused on one remaining "troublemaker." He was Big Foot, chief of a band of Miniconjou Lakotas on the Cheyenne River Reservation. Although he was a resister in the spirit of Sitting Bull and Crazy Horse, Big Foot was known to prefer the use of diplomacy rather than fighting.

When news of Sitting Bull's murder reached the chief, he was camped on the Cheyenne River, on his way to his reservation's agency for the distribution of government rations. Big Foot had more than three hundred followers in his band, two thirds of them women and children. The group was nearly out of food, and they were poorly clothed for the harsh winter weather. They did not have enough tipis for shelter. Armed with mostly old rifles and shotguns, the men had no intention of going to war.

Sitting Bull's death shocked and frightened Big Foot. Soon some thirty-eight Hunkpapa refugees from the murdered chief's band joined the group of Miniconjous. Big Foot was no longer sure that going to the Cheyenne River Agency was the right thing to do. Perhaps the band should go to the agency at Pine Ridge where Red Cloud, the Oglala chief, was friendly with the U.S. government. He could offer protection to the Miniconjous.

Meanwhile, an army detachment of the Eighth Cavalry, led by Lieutenant Colonel Edwin V. Sumner, was sent to track Big Foot's movements and to arrest the chief if he did not return to his agency. On December 22, Sumner caught up with Big Foot and ordered him to turn back. Big Foot agreed to go, and the band was escorted by Sumner's troops. As the group neared the Miniconjous' village, Big Foot asked that the women and children not be forced to continue the journey to the agency. He promised Sumner that once he got his people settled in their village, he would come to the agency the next day.

Sumner was troubled. He had been ordered to arrest Big Foot if the chief refused to come in. Should Sumner trust Big Foot to keep his word? The officer had dealt with the chief before and knew him to be a man of peace. Besides, if he captured Big Foot now, there could be trouble, since other Sioux were still at large in the Badlands. Sumner returned to his camp at Standing Rock Agency without the Miniconjou leader.

That night Big Foot conferred with the other male elders in his band. The chief wanted to keep his promise to Sumner, but he was overruled by his council. The others did not trust the army and felt the band should leave for Pine Ridge immediately.

When Big Foot did not show up at the army camp, a worried Sumner sent out his scouts. They discovered that the Miniconjous had fled their village. Sumner held out hope that Big Foot was on his way to the agency, but General Miles, hearing that the chief had not been captured, was furious. He moved to have Sumner

*Big Foot's band of Miniconjou Sioux, shown here in
ceremonial costume, camped on the Cheyenne River in
South Dakota in August 1890. Just four months later, almost
everyone in this photograph would die at Wounded Knee.*

*It was at a council meeting like the one shown in this
painting that Big Foot tried to convince his followers to cooperate
with Lieutenant Colonel Sumner and return to the agency.*

court-martialed for disobeying orders, but Sumner was later cleared of any wrongdoing.

Under cover of night Big Foot's band had set out. It was bitterly cold, and the icy winds stung the Sioux and cut right through their light clothing. It would be a long and difficult journey of 150 miles (241 kilometers) through the Badlands, with only the stars and prayers to the Great Spirit to guide them. At first the band moved swiftly, entering the Badlands on December 24. On Christmas Day, Big Foot sent a message to Pine Ridge Agency: "We are coming in peace."

Soldiers were now scouring the area in search of the Miniconjous. On December 26 the Seventh Cavalry, commanded by Major Samuel M. Whitside, was sent out from Pine Ridge Agency. Whitside was given four troops of soldiers and two powerful cannons called Hotchkiss guns. Whitside's Indian scouts combed the valleys, looking for Big Foot and his band.

The Indians' progress had slowed, for Big Foot had become ill with pneumonia. Food had run out, and the men had begun hunting for game at night, using knives and lariats to avoid being seen or heard. The Indians were even forced to slaughter some of their horses for food, which Big Foot insisted be given to the mothers and infants in the group.

Big Foot knew he could not go much farther. At sunrise on December 28, an advance party of his band met Whitside's scouts and delivered a message from the chief: "I am on my way into your camp." Not trusting Big Foot, Whitside ordered his 235 men into battle formation and marched to meet the approaching Miniconjous. Whitside intercepted the Indian band, which was led by the chief's rickety wagon. A white flag of peace was tied to its side.

Inside, Big Foot, his head wrapped in scarves, attempted to sit up to greet Whitside. His voice was a raspy whisper, and blood dripped from his nose onto his blankets and into frozen puddles on the wagon floor. Through an interpreter, Whitside ordered Big Foot to surrender. The chief was too weak to resist. In the Lakota language, he said that he was leading his people to Pine Ridge Agency and that he did not plan to cause any trouble.

Whitside told Big Foot that he and his followers would be allowed to continue their journey the next day, but tonight they must camp at Wounded Knee. Big Foot was lifted into an army ambulance wagon.

The procession began its descent into Wounded Knee valley, a narrow strip of land bordered by pine-covered ridges. At the head of the line were two cavalry troops. Next came the ambulance and army wagons, followed by the Sioux. Bringing up the rear were two more troops and a pair of Hotchkiss guns.

Big Foot's people were exhausted and near starvation. The men were gaunt, the aged Indians stooped and frail. Their clothing was dirty and ragged. The Indians seemed spiritless as they trudged into the valley.

Although the Sioux were in poor condition and Whitside's troops outnumbered the males in the Indian band, the major sent a request to Pine Ridge Agency for reinforcements. A reply from General Brooke revealed the fate of the Miniconjous. They were to be marched to Nebraska and loaded onto a train bound for Omaha—and prison.

9

THE DEATH OF THE DREAM

Wounded Knee Creek, which the Sioux called Chankpe Opi Wakpala, was approximately 20 miles (32 kilometers) from Pine Ridge Agency. When the procession reached the encampment, the Indians were issued extra tents by the army and told to set up camp near the creek. Rations were distributed and the horses sent out to graze.

The bugler sounded taps, and silence fell over the camp. In the tipis, the Sioux men talked quietly, long into the night. They could hear the click of the soldiers' rifles and the crisp commands of the officers to the lines of cavalrymen surrounding the Indians.

The Sioux were frightened. As he lay in his tent, Big Foot prayed to the Great Spirit that this would be the last day his people would suffer at the hands of the U.S. government.

During the night the rest of the Seventh Cavalry arrived from Pine Ridge Agency, and Colonel James Forsyth took over command. Now the army had a total of 460 officers, soldiers, and artillerymen, plus some forty Oglala scouts. Traveling with them were

Colonel James W. Forsyth, who commanded the Seventh Cavalry and led the attack at Wounded Knee Creek, was inexperienced with Indian relations.

a Catholic priest and three newspaper reporters. Most of the officers had served in previous Indian campaigns. Forsyth, however, had never been a commander in an engagement with the Indians, and the majority of his enlisted men had little or no fighting experience. Nearly one fifth of them were brand-new recruits.

No one will ever know for certain what caused the confrontation to become bloody. Some say the army officers, who had celebrated Big Foot's capture the night before with a keg of whiskey, wanted revenge for Custer's defeat at Little Bighorn. They may have realized that several of the Sioux men in the camp had been warriors in the battle. Others believe the incident resulted from the tension and suspicion that grew on both sides as the soldiers tried to take weapons away from the Sioux.

A cold winter morning that had dawned peacefully ended in death and destruction. The fighting was horrible. Soldiers fired point-blank at mostly unarmed Indians. As dozens of exploding shells rained on the Indian camp, many Sioux rushed for protection into a ravine that ran west of the creek. Some of the women frantically dug hollows in the banks of the gully in which to hide their infants, but artillery fire caved in the earth and tore through the helpless mothers and babies.

Many other Sioux men, women, and children, fleeing for their lives, were hunted down and slaughtered a few miles from the site of the massacre. Years later an army officer would recall that, within what seemed like moments, "there was not a living thing before us, warriors, squaws, children, ponies, dogs . . ."

The wounded Sioux who were removed from the field and carried to Pine Ridge Agency were made to lie freezing, in open wagons until space could be found for them inside. Many died. The agency's mission chapel was turned into a hospital, its benches removed and its floor covered with straw. Over the pulpit was a banner, part of the chapel's Christmas decorations. Its message was ironic: PEACE ON EARTH, GOOD WILL TO MEN.

The final toll at Wounded Knee was 153 Sioux dead and 44 seriously wounded, counted on the site. But many more victims had either been taken away by other Sioux who arrived after the massacre or had crawled off, to die later from their injuries.

This woman and her children survived the massacre
at Wounded Knee, but she was shot fourteen times
and her children were both wounded.

On New Year's Day 1891 the blizzard had ended, and a burial detail was sent to the site. It included soldiers and a number of civilians, some of whom had been offered two dollars for every corpse they retrieved and buried. Between the creek and the ravine dozens of snow-covered mounds hid bodies that were torn and bloody. Most were frozen in grotesque positions that told of the victims' agonizing deaths.

The corpses were stripped for souvenirs. Ghost Shirts were particularly coveted items. The bodies were loaded onto wagons like logs. A rectangular pit, 50 feet by 6 feet by 6 feet (roughly 15 by 2 by 2 meters), was dug, and into it the dead Sioux, including Big Foot, were dumped without caskets, prayers, or any kind of ceremony. Before shoveling dirt over the mass grave, the burial party posed beside the pit for a photograph.

The army's explanation for the incident was that Indian "treachery" had triggered a fierce "battle." The thirty dead soldiers were buried with full military honors. Congressional Medals of Honor for heroism were awarded to three officers and fourteen soldiers of the Seventh Cavalry.

General Miles, however, called for a court-martial of Forsyth, charging that the officer had endangered his men and needlessly killed Indian women and children. Forsyth was temporarily relieved of his command but was later found innocent of the charges by the secretary of war. General Miles also requested that restitution be made by Congress to the Sioux survivors of Wounded Knee. The proposal came up for discussion repeatedly over the next twenty years but was never approved.

The Ghost Dance religion died out. Wounded Knee proved that the Ghost Spirits could not protect the Sioux. And as spring came and went, the Indians realized Wovoka's prophecy would not

Wounded Knee II

Wounded Knee has come to symbolize all the injustices suffered by Native Americans at the hands of the U.S. government. In the hundred years since the massacre, the struggle for Indian rights has continued.

On February 28, 1973, some two hundred to three hundred Native Americans, militant members of the American Indian Movement (AIM), seized the village of Wounded Knee to protest poor living conditions on their reservations, particularly at Pine Ridge Reservation. With armored cars and machine guns, the Indians kept more than three hundred soldiers, FBI agents, and tribal police at bay for seventy-one days. Two Indians were killed, and the village was heavily damaged before the protesters surrendered on May 8.

Wounded Knee II, as it came to be called, achieved little for Native Americans. But it called attention to their plight and demonstrated that, despite years of hardship and white domination, the Indian spirit was still alive.

be fulfilled. For a while, small groups of Indians who had been coming in from the Badlands when the massacre took place harassed wagon trains and troop detachments. But some eight thousand soldiers had been mustered in the event of an uprising. There was no more violence. In 1891 the Federal Census Bureau no longer needed to designate a frontier of settlement on the Plains. The conquest of the Indians was final.

When Wovoka learned of the massacre, he abandoned his mission as savior of the native people. "Today, I call upon you to travel a new trail," he is said to have told his followers, "the only trail now open—the white man's road."

In 1907 the Sioux placed a fence around the mass grave at Wounded Knee and erected a monument. It reads in part: "Big Foot was a great chief of the Sioux Indians. He often said, 'I will stand in peace till my last day comes.' "

Descendants of Big Foot and his followers live on the Cheyenne River Reservation in central South Dakota. The site of the Wounded Knee massacre is on Pine Ridge Reservation in southwestern South Dakota and is open to the public.

A photograph taken in 1891 shows wooden sticks marking the graves of the Native Americans killed in the massacre at Wounded Knee.

Chronology

1851   Treaty signed at Fort Laramie, guaranteeing the Indians protection from settlers and providing annual payments in return for their promise to stay within set boundaries.

1854   "Grattan Affair": Conquering Bear and Lieutenant Grattan killed in dispute over cow.

1855   "Harney's Revenge": eighty-six Sioux killed and seventy women and children captured.

1863   War for the Bozeman Trail.

1865   "Fetterman Incident": surprise attack on the Sioux leaves Fetterman and his men dead.

1868   New treaty signed at Fort Laramie; the Sioux agree to move to a reservation; the government agrees to abandon development of the Bozeman Trail and the forts along it.

1873–74   U.S. army expeditions into the Black Hills.

1876	Custer defeated at the Battle of Little Bighorn.
1877	Sitting Bull seeks protection in Canada.
	Crazy Horse surrenders, then is killed.
1881	Sitting Bull surrenders and is taken prisoner.
1883	Sitting Bull is returned to Standing Rock Agency on the Great Sioux Reservation.
1887	The Dawes Act is introduced, taking 100 million acres (nearly 40.5 million hectares) from the Sioux for white settlement.
1889	The Great Sioux Reservation is divided, without Sitting Bull's agreement.
	The Ghost Dance religion is started.
1890	U.S. army troops arrive to control the Ghost Dancing.
	Sitting Bull is murdered while being taken into custody by U.S. officials.
	Big Foot's arrest is ordered.
	Big Foot and his followers are intercepted on their way to the army camp at Pine Ridge Agency.
	Massacre at Wounded Knee: more than two hundred Sioux killed.

Further Reading

Brown, Dee. *Wounded Knee: An Indian History of the American West* (*Bury My Heart at Wounded Knee* adapted for young readers). New York: Holt, Rinehart and Winston, 1974.

The Earth Is Sore: Native Americans on Nature. Adapted and illustrated by Aline Amon. New York: Atheneum, 1981.

Eisenberg, Lisa. *The Story of Sitting Bull.* New York: Parachute Press, 1991.

Luling, Virginia. *Indians of the North American Plains.* London: MacDonald Educational Co., 1978.

Neihardt, John G. *Black Elk Speaks.* Lincoln: University of Nebraska Press, 1961.

Osinski, Alice. *The Sioux.* Chicago: Childrens Press, 1984.

Utley, Robert. *Indian, Soldier and Settler.* St. Louis: Jefferson National Expansion Historical Association and National Park Service, 1979.

Waldman, Carl. *Atlas of the North American Indian.* New York: Facts On File Publications, 1985.

Waldman, Carl. *Encyclopedia of Native American Tribes.* New York: Facts On File Publications, 1988.

Wolfson, Evelyn. *The Teton Sioux: People of the Plains.* Brookfield, Conn.: The Millbrook Press, 1992.

$\mathcal{S}ources$

Sources for *Death of a Dream: The Massacre at Wounded Knee* included reference books, histories, and Native American biographies, autobiographies, periodicals, poetry, and oral histories. Particularly helpful were the recollections of James H. McGregor, a superintendent at Pine Ridge in the 1930s, published as *The Wounded Knee Massacre, from the Viewpoint of the Sioux* and in the collection of the American Indian Archeological Institute in Washington, Connecticut.

Of special interest were newsletters published by the Eagle Wing Press, Inc., in Naugatuck, Connecticut, and the American Indians for Development in Meriden, Connecticut, commemorating the one hundredth anniversary of the massacre.

Robert M. Utley's books on Native Americans, including *The Last Days of the Sioux Nation*; Alvin M. Josephy, Jr.'s *Now That the Buffalo's Gone*; and Ralph K. Andrist's *Last Days of the Plains Indians* provided important background for the Wounded Knee story.

Peter Matthiesson's *In the Spirit of Crazy Horse* offered a compelling chronicle of the long conflict between the Lakota people and the U.S. government, through Wounded Knee II. And, of course, an invaluable source was *Bury My Heart at Wounded Knee*, Dee Brown's moving account of the struggle by Native Americans to preserve their homeland and way of life on the Great Plains.

A complete list of sources follows.

Ambrose, Steven E. *Crazy Horse and Custer.* New York: Doubleday & Co., 1975.

American Indians for Development Newsletter. Meriden, Conn.: AIM Publications, Nov.–Dec. 1990.

Andrist, Ralph K. *The Long Death: The Last Days of the Plains Indian.* New York: Macmillan Co., 1964.

Brown, Dee. *Bury My Heart at Wounded Knee.* New York: Henry Holt and Co., 1970.

Brown, Dee. *The Westerners.* New York: Holt, Rinehart and Winston, 1974.

Carroll, John M., ed. *Custer's Chief of Scouts.* Lincoln: University of Nebraska Press, 1987.

Curtis, Edward S. *The North American Indian.* New York: University Press, 1930.

Deloria, Vine, Jr. *Behind the Trail of Broken Treaties.* New York: Delacorte Press, 1974.

The Eagle. Naugatuck, Conn.: Eagle Wing Press, Nov.–Dec. 1990.

The Earth Is Sore: Native Americans on Nature. Adapted and illustrated by Aline Amon. New York: Atheneum, 1981.

Eisenberg, Lisa. *The Story of Sitting Bull.* New York: Parachute Press, 1991.

Engel, Lor. *Among the Plains Indians.* Minneapolis: Lerner Publications, 1970.

Freedman, Russell. *Indian Chiefs.* New York: Holiday House, 1987.

Haines, Francis. *The Plains Indians.* New York: Thomas Y. Crowell Co., 1976.

Jackson, Helen Hunt. *A Century of Dishonor.* New York: Harper & Row, 1965.

Josephy, Alvin M., Jr. *Now That the Buffalo's Gone.* New York: Alfred A. Knopf, 1985.

Josephy, Alvin M., Jr. *The Patriot Chiefs.* New York: Viking Press, 1961.

Luling, Virginia. *Indians of the North American Plains*. London: MacDonald Educational Press, 1978.

Matthiesson, Peter. *In the Spirit of Crazy Horse*. New York: Viking Press, 1983.

Matthiesson, Peter. *Indian Country*. New York: Viking Press, 1984.

Maxwell, James A., ed. *America's Fascinating Indian Heritage*. New York: Reader's Digest Association, Inc., 1978.

McGregor, James H. *The Wounded Knee Massacre, from the Viewpoint of the Sioux*. Baltimore: Fenwyn Press, 1940.

Neihardt, John G. *Black Elk Speaks*. Lincoln: University of Nebraska Press, 1961.

Osinski, Alice. *The Sioux*. Chicago: Childrens Press, 1984.

Rachlis, Eugene. *Indians of the Plains*. New York: American Heritage Junior Library, 1960.

Standing Bear, Luther. *My People, the Sioux*. Lincoln: University of Nebraska Press, 1975.

Tebbel, John, and Jennison, Keith. *The American Indian Wars*. New York: Bonanza Books, 1960.

Turner, Frederick W., III. *The North American Indian Reader*. New York: Viking Press, 1974.

Underhill, Ruth Murray. *Red Man's America*. Chicago: University of Chicago Press, 1953.

Utley, Robert M. *Indian, Soldier and Settler*. St. Louis: Jefferson National Expansion Historical Association and the National Park Service, 1979.

Utley, Robert M. *The Last Days of the Sioux Nation*. New Haven: Yale University Press, 1963.

Waldman, Carl. *Atlas of the North American Indian*. New York: Facts On File Publications, 1985.

Waldman, Carl. *Encyclopedia of Native American Tribes*. New York: Facts On File Publications, 1988.

Wellman, Paul I. *Death on Horseback*. Philadelphia: J. B. Lippincott Co., 1947.

The World of the American Indian. Washington, D.C.: National Geographical Society, 1974.

Index